What Gypsies Don't Know

What Gypsies Don't Know

A Collection of Poems

Natalie Lobe

Washington, DC

Copyright © 2018 by Natalie Lobe

New Academia Publishing 2018

All rights reserved. No part of this book may be reproduced or transmitted in any form or by any means, electronic or mechanical, including photocopying, recording, or by any information storage and retrieval system.

Printed in the United States of America

Library of Congress Control Number: 2018949414
ISBN 978-0-9995572-6-6 paperback (alk. paper)

 An imprint of New Academia Publishing

 New Academia Publishing
4401-A Connecticut Avenue NW #236, Washington DC 20008
info@newacademia.com - www.newacademia.com

For Nathan and Jonas
Harbingers of the future

Contents

Murmurs Underground	1
Had There Been Snow	3
Pangs	4
Roots	5
Opposing Forces	6
In The Last Act	7
Pineapple Love Song	8
Secrets	9
An Almost Impossible Friendship	10
Poems, Books and Yarn	11
Winged Victory	12
Dear Mom	13
Pantoum of the Round Table	14
Assonance	16
Four Leaf Clovers	17
Hummingbird	18
To a Diviner	19
Quantum	20
Virtual Dimensions	21
In Praise of Uncertainty	22
The Gallery	23
Sculpture in Usha's Living Room	24
Good Hands	25
Cello	26

Adagio	27
Lot's Wife	28
Fragrance	29
What Gypsies Don't Know	30

The Plain Blue Truth — 31

The Sump Pump	33
Blackberry Picking	34
Translation	35
Rain	36
Flood	37
Nesting	39
Cardinals	40
Bird Feeder Rondo	41
Travelers Advisory	42
Curling	43
Cantal, France	44
Rendezvous with Myself	45
Northern Lights	46
The Poets' Prompt	47
How It Works	48
Aftermath	49
Dreaming in the Cold	50
Namesake	51
Loss	52
Folded Triangles	53
Monuments	54
Mandolin	56
Autumn	57
Love Sounds	58
Special Delivery, 1958	59

Bird Tails	60
Freedom	61
At the Ice Rink	62
About Walls	63
Sunrise	64
The Ghost of Henrietta Lacks	65
Because I Don't Know How to Say It	66
Saying Goodbye	68

Acknowledgements   71

MURMURS UNDERGROUND

Had There Been Snow

Walking a trail of flat, brown underbrush
lined with maple and tulip poplar limbs,
dead leaves and acorns crunching underfoot,
your fingers go numb with the cold.

Feathered stems of dry goldenrod, gray rocks
piled beside a fence, the stump of an oak
struck down last summer, affirm your place
and season. Branches without leaves,

sticks without sap recall the trophies
and scars from yesterday, decades ago
or some time in between, as you trudge
parallel to the interstate highway.

Had there been snow, the sharp edge of chill
would be polished smooth to the universal
everyness of white mounds, ghost figures
stretching farther back than any tree dare go.

No rubble, no landmarks would mar the white.
Unencumbered, you would place your foot
in the snow to make your initial mark,
one boot print away from starting fresh.

Pangs

I fancy myself an artist drawing a barn.
One horizontal line for the floor
slopes so precipitously the poor cows
will slide south and their milk will sour.
I should have used a straight-edge but
no, I was in too much of a rush.

A vertical line for the side of the building
is perfect until I have an urge
to wiggle my finger, making crevices
where the hay will stick—smell foul.
Everyone will point to my barn and snicker,
Bad job. No control.

I erase one crooked line to a black smudge.
This makes a hole with a crenulated edge.
I try to make it flat with my thumbnail
but the hole grows bigger, the paper so thin
I cannot mask the scar.

I am careful with the roof: measure the angles
and balance the sides. My charcoal shingles
are tight, one against the other. What good
is a leak-free roof on a foundation too flimsy
to bear the unbearable weight.

I think about the innocent cows: sisters,
daughters, mothers, aunts. Their trust gone
amuck. I could have done it right,
I could have drawn sturdy posts and beams
with a thick lead on smudge-resistant paper.

So much depended on me.

Roots

On Bald Island, North Carolina, our naturalist
stops at an uncultivated patch of scrub-growth,
points to a plant, non-descript among the non-descript.

This little fella's a transplant from New Jersey.
Every spring it moves a little bit west toward Jersey,
not even an inch.

I have read that oysters taken from Connecticut
to Chicago take on "high tide behavior," as if Illinois
had its own Midwestern ebb and flood.

And how some "Conversos," Jews forced to the Cross
twenty generations ago, still light candles every Friday
night in the basement, hidden from outsiders.

Ask them why and they say, *We just do.*
After dinner, Mother slips downstairs to tamp the flames,
a gold cross dangling at her throat.

Opposing Forces

Limestone makes sense to poets and sages
who praise a changing landscape
until even death takes on the cosmos.
I cannot imagine any more than they
a faultless love without the murmur
of underground streams.

But one that endures the cross currents,
the rip tides – that's another kettle of fish.
As love pricks holes in blood vessels
taut with desire, the hardy side laughs,
offers a clumsy caress or stumbles
into a crevice, appearing, disappearing
with the flick of fidelity, a turn of the eye.

If anvil and hammer cannot mold love
the twisting has its own reality.
The hand that flings a terra cotta,
smashing it to the ground, reassembles
piece by piece unable to quell the doing.

In The Last Act

she is clinging to Rudolpho,
her arms the color of bone. He cradles
her smallness like a sand dollar
ready to break any minute.
A potion for her cough, a muff,
woolen coat to still the trembling.
Ah, Mimi, he cries. Outside,
a group of revelers with strong lungs
and crimson scarves hail the New Year.
Spring, no more than illusion, hovers
in the wings as the two lovers
fill the tiny garret with passionate song.
She recalls, in sunset tones, the day
she knocked on his door: lost key,
flickering candle, a sip of wine,
a modest blush. *Mi chiamano Mimi.*
The orchestra thunders, she crumples
onto the couch, the curtain falls.
Once more we cry, *Brava, Brava,*
for Mimi's immortal death.

Pineapple Love Song

Pineapple wraps its hexagons
around a yellow belly.
Through a barbed crust
the seep of ambrosia
envelops us.

Underneath the rounds and squares
pale from years and washings
the old quilt hides
the thrashing of lovers
their muffled cries.

Just below the furrowed skin
lined deeper every winter
red blood runs
like a hot spring seething
underground.

Wrapped inside your tangled form
arms, buttocks, thighs,
your embrace
rekindles embers
sets me ablaze.

Secrets

Every secret is a restless thing,
frets like a hornet beating
on the window pane.
Leave me alone, you want to cry,
Stay hidden. Leave me in peace.

But it pries and pushes, unlocks
your will, mocks your resolve,
outs itself. A secret revealed
may bring on shock, despair,
relief—or just fizzle
like a firecracker in the rain.

An Almost Impossible Friendship

Not far from the border at Gaza lies an indifferent sea,
tide brushing war-torn shores, sand riddled with alien shells.

From opposite sides, a friendship thrives
like a marsh rose in the desert. Maha, the Arab,
and Roni, the Jew, phone and text all day. *Are you coping?*

Roni works a farm 800 yards from the border.
Maha, a translator, shares a flat in Gaza City.
They met when Maha crossed over for medical help.
No one crosses now, except soldiers with grenades.

Their countrymen sneer, *Friends? That cannot be.*
The women persevere. Sometimes they are afraid.

I think they dream of sipping tea in the quiet
of an afternoon, watching children play on the beach,
laughing about the foibles of an ordinary day.

Today, it is the blip of a cell phone and thin voices
barely heard above the sirens and screams,
Take care, my friend. Take care.

Poems, Books and Yarn

The shop on Maryland Avenue is a duo.
Shelves of books on one side,
shelves of yarn on the other.
Today, the shop is hosting safety pin poets
reading protest poems. Inauguration looms in days.
The poets call for compassion, love, justice,
denounce the bigots, the fat cats, the jingoes.

Balls of yarn stacked in pastel shades
like giant bon-bons add color, texture to the scene.
Silent stacks of books in venerable covers
hold centuries of wisdom between front and back.
Sitting on the yarn side, I finger a ball of pink alpaca
and wonder if the soft wool absorbs some of the rage.

Otherwise, the room is electric with the voices,
white, tan, brown-skinned poets hoping for hope,
unwinding like yarn balls their visions of what's to come:
division, despair, hypocrisy, hate —books, scarves, socks?

Winged Victory

Picture a third grade class, decades ago, in a four-room schoolhouse.
Connecticut's cold winter keeps the kids from outside recess.
Instead, they relay race past ink stained desks—a ruler for a baton.

Picture me, round-face, corkscrew curls, last one chosen
for anyone's team. With lisle hose rumpling down my legs,
I stand and wait, least wanted, a cipher in the math of self-esteem.

I listen to fortune murmur, "Luck helps those who help themselves."
In the back of Auntie's closet, I find a pair of dusty shoes,
brown suede, rubber soles, light as the lady slipper growing outside.
Auntie's so small and I am so tall they fit like a layer of skin.

Next day at school, in Auntie's shoes, my fortune lies in suede.
When recess comes, I grab the baton, think YES and start to run.
I know how it feels to have wings on your heels, moving like a gazelle.

Up and down the aisles I fly, a vapor trail of chalk-dust following behind.
I am leading my team by 20 desks. We are going to win.
I plunk the baton on teacher's desk. Picture me now.

Dear Mom

Grandma said you were free
like a bird, maybe a swan
your neck was so long.
When you ran on the beach, paddled
your beloved *Old Town*, danced
the fox trot, heads turned,
suitors gathered.

Then you, the expert swimmer,
joined hands and dove
into the suburbs with Dad,
made me and Jim. You tugged us in
to your crammed-full days:
the zoo, the park, the boat lake
and stories at twilight.

If only you'd had warning
but death, never thoughtful
came storming through
the shutters and wrecked our home.
You screamed and tore apart
your widow's veil while
Jim and I stood silent.

Sinking in a flood of grief
you filled a dozen years
with tears, drenched
your black dresses, washed away
the child I was for a woman
who could not cry.

Pantoum of the Round Table

We sit at the table, which is oak and round:
Grandpa, Nana, Auntie, my mom the widow and me.
A family linked with tenuous strands,
maybe electromagnets in the claw feet.

Grandpa, Nana, Auntie, the widow and me.
Only red blood could bind us together, or maybe
electromagnets inside the table's claw feet.
"Please pass the lamb chops," says Auntie.

Only red blood could bind us—or else
the fat from the meat, acting like glue.
"Please pass the chops," Auntie asks.
Plates full of food are nothing new.

The fat from the chops is as thick as glue,
but it's the widow's favorite—she eats it with relish.
Plates full of food are nothing new,
nor starting to talk when hunger's diminished.

Eating her food with less and less relish
the widow laments that life is so hard.
(Conversation starts when hunger's diminished.)
"Nonsense," says Nana, "I think you're bored."

The widow laments that life is so hard
without her beloved husband and mentor.
Nana says, "Nonsense, I think you're bored."
The widow gets teary; her voice goes louder.

Without her beloved husband and mentor
the widow cries, "You don't understand."
As she becomes teary her voice grows louder.
"Stop it, please," Grandpa commands.

The widow hollers, "You never understand."
She storms from the table in a flood of tears.
"Stop it, now," Grandpa commands.
I lower my head, wish for plugs in my ears.

The widow storms from the table in tears.
"Now go to your mother," Nana commands.
I lower my head, wish for plugs in my ears.
Then leave the table, oak and round.

Assonance

Snakes don't bother refugees
so I escape my mother's moans,
(a widow's tears can drown)
roll over the stone wall, brush my thighs
with poison oak on Old Mohegan Trail.

I stalk the path for Solomon's seal,
Jack-in-the-pulpit, an arrowhead nuzzled
in Connecticut soil. Thickets and briars
line the trail. My feet swish rhythms
in brown leaves, the errant child dancing
solo on sacred ground, crouching beside
pine and birch with a jumble of roots
thrust from the dirt. What blooms?

A yellow wild orchid, not to be touched,
Indian pipe, black at the touch, rocks stuffed
with columbine (my mother's favorite.)
How it bends. Supplication?

I chew on a sarsaparilla twig and run, run,
embrace the snakes, the trails of bittersweet
spilling spitfire tears—dry as my own.

Four Leaf Clovers

Like an egret after a snail
you, my long-necked mother
dove into the lawns, pastures,
fields of Connecticut
to pluck one four-leaf clover
from among a million threes.

You pressed each green treasure
between frayed pages
in *The Hebrew Book of Prayer*
where faith met luck in a Kadish
read at the husband's grave.

Now the clovers are brittle and pale,
their stems and veins still firm.
The middle of the book where leaves
press best, last the longest
is like your own immortality

which came, not at the end
but the middle green years
when you seized from the grass
your four leafed charms,
your tokens of hope.

Hummingbird

Flashes of green, red, black
at my bird feeder
whirl in a dizzy blur
as if the crown jewels
had sprouted wings.
The bird, mindless
of my human hulk
just an arm's length away,
fuels up on sugar water
preparing for the long flight
across the continent,
over the Gulf to Mexico
in time to breed
a new generation:
undaunted Davids,
pioneers of wind.

To a Diviner

You sniff at the edges of tarot cards
like mice casing a slab of cheese.
You sink your teeth in tomorrow,
seeking omens sliced by light and dark,

play Russian Roulette with crystal die,
Eureka, doomsday, but minutes away!
You favor the stars with omniscience,
ignore Diogenes, his lantern in hand.

What to believe and what to cast out
or abandon like a doomed poem?
Evaporation, not annihilation seems
more suited to the theater of mystique.

Yet, to be certain I don't miss a signal,
I say, "Come, look at my palm."

Quantum

Quantum theory goes like this:
probability rules the universe—
I get it; *life is a crapshoot.*
Give it a roll and you win or you lose.

One guy's a genius *and* a football star,
his brother is in the loony bin.
One has a "Jag" and girlfriends galore.
Another rides a bus, has warts.

Your mom gets cancer at age fifty-three,
your sister takes off in the pale of the moon,
your big graduation but Dad doesn't come.
The quantum momentum is on.

If you don't take to quantum, feel stuck
like Job—try faith in the wisdom of God,
Allah, Buddha, Jesus or Zeus,
whatever can better your odds.

Virtual Dimensions

I dream in 3D.
I have met and conquered *blue tooth*,
float like an angel in *cloud*,
text faster than the speed of light,
make *twitter* my second language.
In my high tech imagination
the stars of Star Wars cover me
in showers of sparkling silver.

Remember we made telephones
with tin cans and wire? If you shouted
the words were clear.

Space turned elastic
pushes the horizon deep—beyond reach,
while the foreground bends like a willow.
I am lying on my back under the pear tree,
caught in a vision so vivid I reach out
to catch the fruit falling mid-air—
nothing in my hand.

In Praise of Uncertainty

When fog envelops
our island the sharp edges
of rock jetties, white sails
toe prints and piper prints
fade like a Cezanne brushed
on a gray canvas of sky.
I crave these days when
definition submits to
uncertainty: the edges
of pain obscured in haze,
waves of anger becalmed
by salty clouds of mist.
While foghorns bellow
along the ocean's coast,
beware of the shallows,
beware of the shoals.
See with your radar
your fingers and toes.

The Gallery

The white church, where Homewood Road turns west,
used to serve the hallelujah folks. Now, patrons
move quietly among the glass shelves and scrutinize

clay pots, bowls, vases, glazed with mauve and gold.
Thin-blown goblets turn light into strips of rainbow.
A galaxy of hand-wrought earrings shines on copper mesh.

The pews are gone, the pulpit and stern cross. Outside
a bell, painted toneless, hovers like an expectant woman
over her precious flock – *Do not break the merchandise.*

Behind the church, not a church, bones rest in peace.
Their granite markers tilt slantwise from the ground
toward their clay counterparts inside.

In a small back room where Reverend wrestled meaning
from Eden or Gomorrah, the potter spins soft mounds of clay
between her palms. She puzzles creation's quirky ways.

Sculpture in Usha's Living Room

A skein of stone
curls from woman to child
their faceless heads unmarred
by ridge or line, spring from a single torso.

The sculpture, polished smooth in whirlpools
of the Niger, makes green reflections on a glass shelf.
In a nearby chair, Usha chisels words
about bonds, permanent as rock.

I say, flesh is another matter
and recreate the figure of my newborn
untethered, first cry and ready to
carve out her self.

Good Hands

I could have been a surgeon, Grandpa said
as he laid his hands on the wide oak arms
of the Morris chair, his favored place to sit.
He and I examined his hands—bloated veins
on the back and deep gullies on the palm
gave them status. I glanced at my own runts,
seamless and pink with dirt in the fingernails.

Grandpa's hands never sewed a gash,
straightened a bone or pulled out an appendix,
but his nuanced strokes with a fountain pen,
his cathedral A's and new moon C's swept
across a piece of paper in pirouette style.

He could miter perfect corners on two by fours,
sand, varnish, sand again until a cut of maple
shone velvet brown. With his chisel poised
between thumb and forefinger, he shaved
tissue-thin ribbons that curled from a plank.
He taught me how to drive a nail straight shot.

After Grandpa died, the Morris chair languished
in our garage for thirty years (who could get rid
of Grandpa's chair.) Then we flushed out
the crickets, restored the cushions, rubbed the wood
until its wide arms glowing in golden oak
stood ready for another pair of good hands.

Cello

Strings
    taut as muscles
  stretched over bone
tremble at the bow's command
     coming from deep within
  burnished wood
    waves of Mozart,
Mendelssohn, Brahms
    wash the green hips
  of countryside
undulating
  like swimmers
    moving downstream.

Adagio

The tempo of an afternoon in mid-August
moves with the languor of a caterpillar
lazing his silent trail in the dirt by my chair.
The branches of the maple tree rustle,
the sound more muted by my failing ears.

Wind waves separate into single strands
of violin, cello, harpsichord,
replace the tempests of yesterday:
cymbals of love, drums of anger,
trumpets of ambition marching
through the early years.

When I was young, death came close:
once with the screeching of brakes,
once with a surgeon's knife.
Then it became a mere distraction
between signals: presto, rondo, overture.
The end was in-between beginnings.

The beginnings have cooled,
transformed into the lyrical songs
that mothers sing to children sing to mothers.
Keep in mind I cannot sing, blow, strum,
or finger the clavichord.
The tapestry of sounds is not my own,
yet I stake my claim.

Lot's Wife

What if
she never looked back.
It being her lot to follow,
she trudges behind Lot
fixing her eye on the fuzz
at the nape of his neck.
A daring woman she is not.

And if
the burning Gomorrah
smelling sulfur and fire
in black fury clouds
makes her crave for the goat
which still cooks in her pot,
she follows her Lot.

What
is ahead she knows not
but question she does not.
Her lot is to obey,
her daughters the same.
How she yearns to turn,
look back, but does not.

When
they reach a mountain,
find a cave, she keeps house,
as is her lot. She has sons,
grows old—dies a nobody.
A legend she is not.
Salt glistens in sun.

Fragrance

Other loves were meant to last.
Ours went long enough.
After the sweetness lost its taste
the brain went on believing.

So slowly did the blossom pale,
so long to shrink and bend,
wither and lose the scent,
it seemed a sudden ending.

Passion's breath was over, spent,
the air grown still and silent,
yet in passing left a fragrance,
faint as not forgetting.

What Gypsies Don't Know

Tulips in yellow and red turbans spring
from the green confines of leaf like gypsies
in carnival clothes. I had planted the bulbs
on a bleak December afternoon when the holly
cast a shadow abbreviated as the winter day.

Still grieving for a love gone cold, I blended
with the colorless landscape, a reminder
the winter solstice had yet to come.

The hard soil was so resistant I strained
to push a trowel deep enough to lay
each bulb, not like a newborn bedded down
with love and warmth, more like an old
crone who turns the sheets cold—yet
I was convinced that one spring day
when my sorrow lessened, gorgeous colors
of sun and fire would emblazon my tiny plot
somehow confounding the dead.

THE PLAIN BLUE TRUTH

The Sump Pump
For Hank

Hard to believe it wasn't last week,
when your brother was still a bulge in my belly,
your sister off to first grade
and, if it was a rainy day, we'd rush

for the basement to watch the sump pump.
How the motor hummed as the floater
rose, then descended like a baton
until the water level dropped to murky depths.

When the motor went mute, we busied ourselves,
upstairs, you eating pretzels, me pushing the vacuum.
Hear it, Mom, you would say. *Let's go, hurry up!*
And we'd fly down the steps for the next round.

The sump pump gave our rainy days structure,
rhythm, thrills like riding a Ferris wheel.
None of my friends did anything like that.
None of my friends had a kid like that.

Forty years later, you're immersed in the workings
of sea monitors, submersibles and other gizmos
bulging with computer chips and black wires.
Me? I'm still in the dark, trying to figure out
how that darn thing kept our cellar dry.

Blackberry Picking

I could have stayed on the porch with a love poem
or a daydream. I could have gone to the beach,
smeared your back with sunscreen, watched a dolphin,
studied your toe print. Gone giddy from choices.

Instead, I'm in a tangle of blackberry thorns,
reaching for a clump of black nodules so heavy the vine sags.
I have to have *that* one and the one behind, even bigger
and those beauties another ten feet into the briars.

Every prize comes at a price: lacerated arms,
bloody shins, stained fingers, mosquitoes and ticks.
I'm a cautious person, comfort my style, but
today I plunge willy-nilly into prickles, pain and itch,

intractably lured by the vision of my
blackberry cobbler bubbling thick juices over
a tawny crust, exhaling hot purple smells.
Have a taste, let it linger, let's call it ours.

Translation

The language of a wind whistling pine
puts me in the spell of spilled dreams
wonder hopping inside a green breeze.

My back yard blessed with messages
no one can translate except perhaps
infants and idiots whose unencumbered
brains know by instinct the readings
of red geraniums, sunsets and maple
boughs bowing down to the ground.

Rustle replaces words and words
acquiesce to the touch of June moss
to the rhythm of raindrops on the awning
to the aroma of lilac and wet grass.
All of which you know and I know
is the plain blue truth.

Rain

A late August shower taps
paradiddle on the porch roof,
saturates my beach towel

flung across the folding chair.
The rainspouts gush narrow waterfalls
and circles explode in the bird bath.

Undaunted, the rose hip, marigold,
zinnias, brush waterproof red,
yellow and gold on a grey canvas.

I cushion down in the corner
of my glider, look at the dunes, orbit
with my planet and ask myself,

What more does the galaxy offer?
Worlds made of burning clouds, dry
lakes, mountains unwashed and cold.

Hardly a match for wet marigolds,
a glider, paradiddle, me and the rain.

Flood

As the TV screen shows torrents of rain
pelting up the Florida coast
spreading havoc farther and farther,
I remember the ark and those aboard,
how the word came down to Noah, an elder
to build himself a mighty vessel,

to labor until he readied the vessel
for forty days and nights of rain.
When his ship was built, Noah the elder
gathered creatures from coast to coast,
two of each species and took them aboard.
This the command of almighty Father.

Two of each kind: a mother, a father,
a civilization inside one vessel,
bellowing, bleating, stomping the boards,
surrounded by water and soaked with rain.
All those creatures left on the coast
now submerged with the cedars and elders.

Jammed together pups and their elders,
scolding, impatient mothers and fathers
despairing of the life inside the vessel
which bobbed and lurched under the rain
like the mighty whale trying to coast
through the waves with Jonah aboard.

Some of them howled, some were bored,
all of them angry at Noah, though elder,
blaming *him* for the deluge of rain.
"Wait," cried Noah, " Our heavenly Father
ordered the rain and this rescue vessel.
I'll send a scout to look for dry coast."

He released a dove to seek a green coast
while all the creatures imprisoned aboard
lamented, "We'll never get out of this vessel."
But the dove flew by with a twig of elder,
or olive—a sign that the almighty father
had kept his promise to end the rain."

From coast to coast, praise Noah, elder
and wiser than all aboard: captain and father
whose vessel survived the ultimate rain.

Nesting

Three weeks ago a mourning dove began
her maternal vigil in my Virginia pine.
I approach, she sits unruffled.
Aren't you afraid of me?

Nesting in another branch, a robin chirps
in rage when I come close. Her mate darts
from branch to branch, cackling bird fury.
I won't hurt you.

Dove and I exchange knowing stares.
We know and robin should know
a coming birth doesn't require all that ruckus.
Robin, be quiet in my tree.

Cardinals

Two fledglings wait
on my porch rail,
their wings quivering
as if too wet for takeoff.
Are they waiting
for a boost of wind?

Afraid to test
the aerodynamics,
or just afraid?
Mother bird flits about,

hovers, primes each
offspring beak to beak
with a safflower seed
plucked from my feeder.
Fly, my darlings,
taste the sky.

Bird Feeder Rondo

                                                Sometimes they show up in droves.
Finches, juncos and cardinals flaming over toothpick toes.
The sunflower seed is ravished, disappears as if a Hoover swept in.

                Some of them stay nameless: The gray one with a spear-beak,
the one in plump brown, his watchful eye looking up and around after each bite.

Woodpeckers prefer suet.
Sporting red yarmulkes, they peck the daylights out of a block of fat. Others,
less flashy but just as hungry work their bills like tiny drumsticks in band practice.

                    Sometimes they fight.
The cardinals and those black birds square it out while the Carolina wrens,
midgets in the bird world, patiently wait their turn.
 A few, like the hummingbirds, stop for respite on the long trip South.

                            Sometimes, like promises, they don't show up at all.

Travelers Advisory

The art of travel is more than longing
for the steps of Xian, the caves of Dordogne,
before you wake to another morning.

You stand in the glow of Sistine's awning,
a tear for the master before you move on,
for the art of travel is more than longing.

You look at Denali as day is dawning,
breathe in the echoes, make them your own,
before you inhale another morning.

Caress the *Wall* and savor returning
to Solomon's shrine—his holy ground.
The art of travel is more than longing.

Dive among coral where sea life is swarming
with yellows and crimsons, as if it were home,
before you wake up to one more morning.

Consider travel the gift of transforming
from what you were to what you've become,
for the art of travel is more than longing
for some new place tomorrow morning.

Curling

Between San Juan and La Par Guerra
I stumble along a trail thick with roots,
ruts and regrets. Slippery stones and mud
challenge the treads of my boots.

Hardly a rhapsodic scene, yet I stop
to admire a nameless flower nestled
like a pink dust ball in a vessel, three
green leaves pointing skyward.

Touch one of the leaves and it curls up,
says the hiker behind me. I touch
the plant and watch while the leaves
shrink into a tiny fist.

Curling keeps you warm and safe
like a caterpillar curled in the sun,
like an unborn floating in the womb,
when I curl against you in bed.

On the other hand, when provoked,
snakes leap out of a curl. The springs
of my grandfather clock activate the hands.
Our baby's hair springs into ringlets,
especially when damp.

Cantal, France

Shades of green color the hillsides.
Pajamas and sheets on clotheslines
flap in the wind like ancestral flags.
Beneath a bridge made of wood slats
cold currents carry *truite* downstream.
Cows munch on wads of grass
and nurse their young.

Castles and chateaus crown the heights,
recalling a specter of knights, steeds, crossbows
and moats hunkering in the valley.
The clink of armor echoes in cowbells
as the animals lumber across the field.

Rendezvous with Myself

It's time I had a get-together with me.
Check the mileage before the odometer breaks,
Wipe down the rusty parts, apply some fresh paint,
BLOW MY HORN and make for the open road.

Northern Lights

A gold scrim washes the Arctic sky
giving a sense of two minds:
reveal/conceal, emblazon/subdue,

The moon, opaque, undefined
like Monet's foggy Giverny—yet
so enhanced as to mimic the sun.

From the hotel parking lot, I see Andromeda,
the dippers, the whole gold studded set
ready for opening night in Reykjavik.

I murmur the silvery words, *Aurora Borealis*,
while each celestial body shimmers in mist:
light and darkness juxtaposed.

Suddenly, the show is over, the curtain down.
An ordinary starlit night takes center stage.
I head back to my numbered room.

The Poets' Prompt

"Write about going to someplace new."
Serendipity! I've just come back from a maiden trip:
not to the beaches of Maui, the snows of the Pole,
the peaks of Denali or the Great Barrier Reef.
Not even Barcelona, dripping Gaudi facades.

My trip was to a surgical office, filled with patients,
none of them young, who sunned too long in bygone days
and now pay homage to the knife. Squares of gauze,
the *haute couture*, grace noses, necks, ears and bald heads.

Mohs — an epidermal tour-de-force — shaves away our skin,
layer by layer until a microscope declares the cancer gone.
Between layers, we wait, in plastic chairs, for the verdict.
We read *Newsweek*, poke our cell phones, stare at the wall.

I look beyond my bandaged nose to my counterparts
and say to myself — this place has its own intrigue.
Call it a shrine, a stop for repairs while sailing to Byzantium.

How it Works (or Does Not)

I have a brand new pen from which the ink flows
like quick-silver. But words come staccato,
hesitate, nudge a comma, balk at the metaphor.
They abandon me and fly from the page
to a Sycamore tree, beneath which golden globes
of wild orchid patiently grow,
their fragile skin glowing like moonrise.

Aftermath

Felled by one of Vermont's worst storms,
white birches lie sideways on forest scrub,
beside clusters of violets and Solomon's seal.
Tree trunks dangle roots as if they were claws
clinging to the last remnants of brown earth
torn from the hollows underneath.

Limbs in skeletal configurations grow
more brittle every day. I walk along the trail
lined with fallen birch trees and think about
another hillside far away in *Blackbirds Field*
where piles of white limbs lie scattered
among the barren rocks. No sounds come from
the charred village: no one left to lament the dead.

Dreaming in the Cold

The temperature plunges to six above zero,
the Bay covered with gray slabs of ice
as if they were tectonic plates risen from below
ready to rebuild a crumbling Earth.

Standing on shore, blue with cold, I say
to the silence, *Let's make another planet
with green fields, sparkling rain and oceans
unblemished as a blue, September sky.*

Let's be the new caretakers who sweep,
plant, nurture, protect the place from enemies
like carbon dioxide, coke bottles, coal dust
and cement, that implacable hater of grass.

While we're at it, let's ship all the guns
to the fiery skies of Venus for forging
into hair pins and frypans so that the women
are beautiful and the sauces gourmet.

Let's say goodbye to the old planet,
now ready for the junk yard, and sing,
sing our own praises for a job well done.

Namesake

The doctor looked at my newborn son sleeping beside me in his cardboard crib and said, Some lively baby, he cries louder than any infant in the nursery! No surprise. The child was named after my father who bounded through his thirty-eight years as if he knew his time was short. I remembered myself at four, jumping from a pier on Long Island Sound, into his strong arms. How we laughed. Did those vigorous genes live on in his namesake?

Maybe not. As if exhausted by his bombastic beginning, my baby slept, turned away from my breast, rarely made a cry. What was wrong? He seemed fragile as an unfledged wren. The nurse looked at his yellow cheeks and said, Jaundice, common in babies, see if you can get him to nurse. Once home he'll pick up.

Once home he did not. What's wrong, I whispered to the doctor, what's wrong? He is fine, the doctor said, perfectly fine, give him a little more time. I watched for change—one, two, three, four, five, six days. In the middle of the sixth night, his face was gray. My imagination? I lifted him from his crib. In the seconds of a lifetime, he turned cold in my arms.

Loss

Howard Benjamin,
our neighbor, went blind
overnight.
He opened his eyes
in the morning
and saw
not his Sadie's pretty face,
nor the red begonia
on the window sill,
not the finch pecking on the feeder,
only black.
All he could do
was push himself
from chair to chair, fumble
with his fork,
grope to find a doorway,
cling to a stair rail.

I'm like that, with you gone.

Folded Triangles

Star-spangled triangles
over red and white stripes
lie on a wood casket.

The widow receives
her three-sided bundle
her hands trembling
like dragonfly wings.

For a moment
the strain of taps
dampens the sounds
of gunshot and groans
bombarding her brain.

Nature offers balance:
scarlet trillium,
lily pads, butterflies,
the peaks of Kilimanjaro,
a spider's web.

The cedars of Lebanon
reaching up to Sagittarius,
its three prongs linked
by fault lines deep enough
not to understand.

Monuments

In a graveyard called *Hope*
Madonnas, pietas and crosses
mingle with life-size statues
on stone pedestals marked
Bertinni, Marzzionne, Peduzzi,
Fazzone: names carried across

the ocean by stonecutters
two hundred years ago
to the State of Vermont.
The tools inside their satchels
would transform great boulders
of granite clinging to the hillsides
into tombstones for the dead.

Everyday life is freeze-framed
along the paths of *Hope*:
a gentleman in an armchair
guards his bones below.
A woman leans toward her man,
bedridden, dying. Pebble tears
mark her cheek, lines of grief
chisel her granite brow.
.
A soldier cut in bas-relief
holds a cigarette and watches
curls of stone smoke waft
across his giant headstone.
A couple in bed, a soccer ball,
an empty chair, a racing car,
a World War I aero plane;
the cortege goes on.

Their mute lips seem to say,
"Look, the unforgotten moments,
the precious stuff of our lives
preserved here on hallowed ground."

I pick up a loose pebble and wonder
what moment would I choose?

Mandolin

After Auntie died I gave away
her miniatures, tiny blown glass
animals without bones or malice,
wooden clogs to fit a kitten's paw,
a gold thimble, a tea-set, cricket size.

I kept one piece—the mandolin,
two inches long, brass, fretted neck,
tuners in place and hair-thin strings.
It lies on my kitchen sill, a reminder
of Auntie.

Her hands are full of *cat's cradle*.
She is offering tootsie rolls and hugs.
I smell her peanuts roasting in the oven.
On the grass out front, Auntie shoots
a croquet ball through the wicket,
smacks the stake. We play jacks
and jump-rope together.

Man-do-lin: The syllables dance on top
of my stove, dos-a-do the fridge,
fill my house with Auntie, her tiny instrument
bulging belly-side up on the kitchen sill.

Autumn

When September removes the curtain
of summer haze and each pebble shines
 sky-blue clear

When brown leaves rustle underfoot,
geese clatter overhead and cricket-song
is swansong

When fiery leaves hover
over clusters of mums the same color

When children, near hidden by backpacks,
climb onto a yellow bus

And when the bittersweet clings to our fence
in a gorgeous disarray of green and cracked-orange

be reminded, *Little time left to love your hardest.*

Love Sounds

Love dances through stanzas
I hold, you croon, I sing, you spin
like dolphins on green waves or

rocket tails on midnight skies
ringing with consonants or
low-toned vowels on soft goose down.

Love plucks words from a tumult
of discordant sounds, transforms them
pizzicato, to a couplet, a tercet

with the heartbeat of a sonnet
the warbling of a villanelle
until the final epitaph,

Without you, my dear — only gibberish.

Special Delivery, 1958

Inside the white room is one bed, one table, one chair and me
in a green smock, big belly rising like a hot air balloon
I am waiting for the next pain and listening to the rain fall
on the city rooftops: the muted tones of popping corn.

Soon I go to the Delivery Room, say goodbye
to my husband who is not allowed to join me for the event.
This will not to be a shared experience but I am not afraid.
I am independent, capable, a woman ahead of her time.

A few hours later, I am back in my white room
sporting a flat profile and a sleepy smile. The sky is clear.
Beside my bed, in a roll-on box is baby girl, my firstborn.
She sleeps in peace after a noisy exit from fetal life.

Right now, it is she and I, fledglings together facing
a fresh new life. I watch her every twitch.
I cannot do otherwise. *Look, world, at my prize!*
But deep down, where you can't see, I'm afraid.

Bird Tails

"To tame a bird, sprinkle salt on its tail," said my best friend in first grade.
I imagined saying, "Gimme your claw," to a sweet yellow finch: then
holding one tiny foot in my hand. Or telling a jay to play dead and watch

the raucous bird lie on his blue side, motionless as an overturned Ked.
I could throw a sunflower seed into the air and order a wren to "fetch."
Off she would go, head bobbing like an old woman.

Salt shaker in hand and hope in my heart I headed for the college campus
close to my home. All afternoon I ran from tree to tree with breadcrumbs
in hand hollering, "Tweet, Tweet," Not even the mocking birds deigned a reply.

I stalked a dove strutting on the grass. He cast me a beady eye, then flew off,
disrupted from an otherwise placid day pecking at candy wrappers on the ground.
I held up a feather snatched from the tarred path. Maybe the owner of the lost tress
would come to make a claim. Then I, the clever one, would get a shot at its tail.

The afternoon cooled, the sun turned west, my stomach churned with hunger.
I let the feather float away and headed for home. Dumb birds—Dumb girl.

Freedom

Of the ten plagues put upon Egyptians
each worse than the one before

the ninth was darkness—not of the place
where the mole finds refuge or the bear

in her deep winter sleep or the black night
holding nuggets of dawn in lightless embrace.

Not even blindness, learning how to compensate
with ear, hand and tongue.

More like a moral eclipse holding
the promise of slaughter tomorrow.

The cravings of slaves to cast away idols,
lashes and ploughs begs the question

which plagues us today. What price freedom,
does it have any bounds?

At the Ice Rink

Hard rock music pierces the frigid air
as steel skates etch circles in rock hard ice
moving clockwise to the rhythms
of "Stairway to Heaven."

Some skaters take long strides. Nonchalant,
they glide with hands at their backs.
Others wobble; wave an arm for ballast,
stumble with ankles bent.

Red, blue, green, white outfits mingle
in a jumble of shapes and movement
like a kaleidoscope being turned
by invisible hands.

The girl in a purple jacket splits
to the center, begins a spin, a dervish blur.
She moves to the rim, circles backwards,
bends, turns, leans forward in purple stardom.

Oblivious to the confines of the rink,
perimeter and diameter, her skates create
elastic space to inhale the freedom
of an unencumbered flight.

About Walls

In Connecticut, the stonewall defines boundaries,
draws a landscape patchworked with squares,
rectangles and a myriad of irregular shapes.
When the settlers cleared the land for growing
they built stonewalls with castaway rock.
Convex on concave became works of art.

They put flat stones on top, not knowing
walking on walls would delight the kids;
"I am not going to fall," I hear myself crowing.
Walking walls gave me a special pleasure
pretending I was a tightrope walker.

I learned, later, that walls have a downside,
(visible or not,) an inside and outside.
Being inside was good but outside a curse.
The odd-ball, the dark skinned, dwarf and Jew,
were ignored, uninvited, taunted and worse.
I, a young Jewess, wished I were not.
The wish was short-lived, the pain a tattoo.

Sunrise

Every night I wage a battle of turns:
side to side, front to back, predictable
as the hands on my bedside clock.
Inside my head, hapless sheep march
in silent circles to stave off the omens,
mishaps of the day turned catastrophic.

When the first trickle of sun slides
through the window blind,
and saffron stripes cross the blanket,
my gymnastics end, soothed
by the scent of morning
and the rumble of automobiles
revving up for the day.

The sun—peacemaker, healer,
makes morning rounds carrying
potions of calm in a silver satchel.
I fall asleep thinking death is not
the shadow but illimitable light,
inviting yet another dawn.

The Ghost of Henrietta Lacks
1920-1952

I know there's a lot of hullabaloo about my cancer cells
after that reporter woman wrote a book about me
so I have come back home where it happened hoping
to clear my head and figure out how I feel.

After all these years away, I don't see much change.
The house, it still looks the same 'cept for the new porch
where you get a good view of that ole muddy crick
that mopes beside our house down to the neighbor's.

Those cancer cells wrenched from my veins got sold
all over the world, even after I was dead. None of my family knew.
You see, my cells are very special—even today they keep living
and growing like a cut-up snake.

Back when my folks were slaves their whole bodies were sold.
I got sold too, in little bits and pieces packed in vials
and I wonder why they did that when I owned those cells.
Maybe because of me being back-of-the bus-colored.

Were they bad people who didn't ask, cheated my kids, my grands?
I kind a think they *meant* right, wanting to help other sick folks,
find a cure, all that. What they did was wrong, but if they are sorry,
well, I have been human too—not now, but I can still figure.

Because I Don't Know How To Say It

Don't go far off even for a day
Because I don't know how to say it: a day is long
And I will be waiting for you as in an empty station
When the trains are parked off somewhere else
Pablo Neruda

When day wanes to shadows,
when twilight's dust spreads
over sycamore branches
like flour sifting into a bowl,
remember the years left behind:
piles of tectonic plates that sway,
crack open and disrupt all the spaces
bound to silence, for we are old,
fragile enough for me to say
Don't go far off not even for a day

Words, lovely upon lovely
hide inside luminescent summers,
unwritten, unsaid, unheard words.
I squandered them and so did you,
doled them out with utmost care.
No profusion of feelings loud or strong,
we choked and spoke of quotidian things:
pot roast and homework and clean-up time.
I wander when you are gone,
Because- I don't know how to say it: a day is long

Think of sap running like a sweet river,
the bark nothing more than a shield
protects an ebullient flow of well- being.
If dryness sets in and roots loosen
like old muscles, not without sensation,
listen for a heartbeat louder than you'd believe,
a cache of words eager for release.
If we could speak just one more time
I'd say, "Look for me on every small occasion."
I will be waiting for you as in an empty station

where naked tracks await their heavy loads
to head for some new destination.
"God Speed," we say, "take your cargo
as we have taken our dreams
to a special garden, some unknown place
hoping to find a niche or a shelf."
The language of passion no longer imprisoned
nor choked in silence will find a way
to track the words within ourselves.
When the trains are parked off somewhere else.

Saying Goodbye

Is easily said to any season, return trip
assured, as if by revolving door.
Let go of success, its grand design
dissolves like a flake of snow.

Youth is superficial except for the angst.
 Give it a wave with no regrets.

Even life itself—ready or not,
farewell is always a given.

But love is not the same. I look at you
And say, *No, it's not the same.*

What smoothes the sharp edges,
crushes the cynic, cannot be dismissed

with a casual wave of the hand
I would chase it like a mindless hound
through briars and rapids, beyond
the ozone even into the black hole,

reach until my arm goes numb,
call until I'm voiceless, but
never, never say "Goodbye."

Acknowledgements

I wish to thank the editors of the publications in which many of the poems first appeared, often in an earlier form. My thanks go to Elisavietta Ritchie and Shirley Brewer for so many useful suggestions on individual poems and their organization in the book. Grace Cavalieri, I cannot thank enough. Without her, it never would happened.

Artword, "Four Leaf Clover."
Blue Unicorn "Let Morning Come," "When the Sun Rises."
California State Quarterly, "In the Last Act," "What Gypsies Don't Know."
Calyx, "Pangs," "Secrets."
Comstock Review, "Assonance," "Because I Don't Know How to Say It."
DIDI Mendez, POETS & ARTISTS Magazine , "Books, Yarn and Poems."
Ekphrasis, a Poetry Journal, "Sculpture in Usha's Living Room."
Evening Street Press, "What Gypsies Don't Know."
Fodderwing, "Aftermath."
G W Review, "Pineapple Love Song."
Gunpowder Review, "Northern Lights," "Good Hands."
Little Patuxent Review, "The Gallery."
Parting Gifts "Had There Been Snow," "Cardinal," "Monuments," "Saying Goodbye," "Quantum."
Poetica, "Darkness."
Scribble, "Had There Been Snow."
Slant, "The Sump Pump."
Studio Potter, "Sculpture in Usha's Living Room."
The Poet's Cookbook, "Blackberry Picking."
Welter, "Dear Mom."

Anthology

"An Almost Impossible Friendship" appeared in the anthology, *The Forgotten Woman*, Grayson Books, 2016.

www.ingramcontent.com/pod-product-compliance
Lightning Source LLC
Chambersburg PA
CBHW031203160426
43193CB00008B/487